MEXICAN BREAD COOKBOOK

Mexican Traditional Recipes for Soft, Sweet, and Savory Breads from Mexico's Bakeries and Home Kitchens

MEXICAN BREAD COOKBOOK
AUTHOR: ELLA ROSE

RECIPE INDEX

INTRODUCTION

I grew up in a small town in America, where freshly baked sliced bread and simple sandwiches were the norm. Though I appreciated the comfort of those classic flavors, I always felt like something was missing. That changed when I took a trip to Mexico a few years ago. On that trip, I was immersed in the sights, sounds, and smells of freshly baked Mexican bread all around me. Each morning, I would stop by the local panadería and take in the incredible aroma. I'd sample pan dulces, conchas, teleras and more, savoring the rich tastes and textures. With each bite, I was transported to bread heaven!

When I returned home, I found myself craving those incredible flavors that had awakened my taste buds. I started testing recipe after recipe to try to recreate those Mexican breads that had captured my heart. After much experimentation, I finally perfected the techniques and ingredients to make authentic Mexican breads like bolillos, tortillas, and molletes completely from scratch.

Now, I want to share the recipes and knowledge I've gained with others who have a passion for Mexican breads like I do. In this cookbook, you'll find my tried and true recipes along with tips and tricks for making these breads just like they do in Mexico. With the proper guidance, you'll be able to fill your own home with the sights, smells, and tastes of fresh Mexican bread anytime you please. So preheat your oven, get out your molcajete, and let's start baking!

ALL ABOUT MEXICAN BREADS

Mexican food is famous worldwide for its delicious flavors. Mexican breads are a great way to enjoy carbs. You can make some at home to satisfy your cravings. There are many tasty Mexican bread recipes to try. Mexican bread comes in many varieties. So it's a popular side dish with main meals. In addition to classic flour tortillas, you can try sweet breads, corn bread, and other wonderful options.

What's the name for Mexican bread?

Despite being in the southern part of North America, Mexican bread is greatly influenced by the French. For instance, the Mexican bolillo developed from the French baguette. The Spanish translation for bread is "pan," which is the term used for bread in Mexico.

Centuries of Experimentation

The history of Mexican bread goes back many centuries. It blends native creativity with European influences. Corn was the main pre-Columbian food. But when the Spanish introduced wheat, baking changed dramatically. Later, French baking methods and customs added even more variety. All these factors created the wonderful diversity of Mexican breads we enjoy today.

A Legacy of Flavor

Mexican breads are still evolving today. They continue long-held traditions but also add new, modern ideas. Some artisan bakers are bringing back old recipes. Other creative bakers try new things. Together, they ensure that Mexican baking has a bright future.

In this cookbook, you will find all kinds of recipes, from traditional to modern. Let's start your baking journey.

Kitchen Measurement Abbreviations Table

Abbreviation	Measurement
Tbsp. tbsp. T.	Tablespoon
Tsp. tsp. t.	Teaspoon
Oz	Ounce
Fl. Oz	Fluid ounce
C.	Cup
Qt.	Quart
Pt.	Pint
Gal.	Gallon
Lb.	Pound
mL	Milliliter
g.	Grams
Kg.	Kilogram
L, l	Liter

1. Besos Pan Dulce (Sweet Bread)

Prep Time: 40 Minutes / Cook Time: 15 Minutes / Resting Time: 30 Minutes / Total Time: 1 Hour 25 Minutes / Yield: 12

Ingredients

- 1 cup of strawberry preserves
- 1/2 teaspoon salt, sifted
- 1 1/2 cups of warm water (110° F), divided
- 1 cup vegetable shortening, melted and cooled
- 4 cups all-purpose flour, sifted
- 1/4 cup of strawberry syrup
- 1/2 cup Imperial Sugar Extra Fine Granulated Sugar
- 2 teaspoons yeast

Instructions

1. In the stand mixer's bowl fitted with a hook attachment, sift together the flour and salt. After adding the shortening, mix on low speed for seven to ten minutes, scraping down the bowl's sides. It should look like wet sand.
2. In a small bowl, mix yeast and one cup of water together. Allow the mixture to sit aside for ten minutes or until it starts to foam.
3. While the mixer is still running, pour in the yeast and water mixture. After adding the remaining water, mix on low for ten minutes or until the dough is smooth and does not stick to the bowl.
4. Take the dough out of the mixer and transfer it to a lightly oiled surface. Knead with your hands for about 5 to 7 minutes. Place in a big bowl and cover with plastic wrap. Take the dough and let it rise for around 30 minutes in a warm place in the kitchen.
5. Punch the dough down and knead it for 5 minutes. Make 24 separate pieces of dough, then roll each into a ball. Place on two large baking sheets, about 2 inches apart. Place clean kitchen towels over the top.
6. Now, heat the oven to 400°F while the dough balls rise. Bake for 13 to 15 minutes, or until the bread's bottoms turn golden brown. The tops will be white. Take it out of the oven. Allow it to cool for five minutes.
7. Put sugar and strawberry syrup in separate shallow bowls on a clean work surface. Gently dip the smooth sides of the bread into the strawberry syrup, then quickly coat them with sugar, moving quickly and carefully. Put it on a plate to serve, and wait a few minutes for the sugar and syrup to set.
8. Put strawberry jam on the flat sides of the bread. Put two pieces of bread together to make a "kiss." Do it again with the other breads. Serve and enjoy.

2. Birotes Salados (Mexican Sourdough Bread)

Prep Time: 1 Hours 20 Minutes / Cook Time: 20 Minutes / Total Time: 1 Hours 40 Minutes / Yield: 5 birotes

Ingredients

Starter Build(311g):

- 3 Tbsp. (36 grams) beer
- 1 egg
- 1/2 cup (100 grams) sourdough starter
- 3/4 cup (100 grams) organic all-purpose flour
- 2 tsp. (10g sugar)
- 1/8 tsp. (1 g salt)
- 1 Tbsp (14 grams) lime juice

Final Dough:

- 2 tsp (11 grams) salt
- 2 cups of (260 grams) whole grain yecora rojo flour
- sourdough starter from above (about 311g)
- 2 cups (260 grams) bread flour
- 1 1/2 cups (345 grams) water

Instructions

Starter Build:

1. Combine the ingredients for the birote sourdough starter three to four hours before you want to mix your dough. If you need more time to build, use less starter and more flour and water instead. (30 grams of water, 40 grams of sourdough starter, and 30 grams of extra flour).
2. Cover and leave the starter to ripen somewhere warm until it has at least doubled in size.

Final dough mixing:

1. In the large bowl, combine all the dough ingredients, including the ripe sourdough starter, and mix until well combined, then cover.
2. Do three sets of stretching and folding the dough over the next hour, with 20-minute rests in between. After just one round, the dough should feel cohesive, with almost nothing coming off your hands. If it's still too wet and doesn't hold together, add 30g (1/4 cup) more flour.
3. Scrape the dough onto the well-floured work surface when it has nearly doubled in size.

To shape:

1. Make a ball out of each of the five or six pieces of dough that you have (237g or 197g).
2. While you flour the linen couche or tea towel where the dough will rise, let the dough rest for a short time.
3. Turn a dough ball over and pinch it into an oval; next, roll it into a tapered tube. Re-roll the tube and sew it more firmly if it still feels loose.
4. After placing the shaped dough seam-side up on the couch, slightly fold the linen to provide support for the dough side. Follow the same steps with all the dough pieces, and then warp with the couche or use another tea towel.

Final proofing and baking:

1. Wait about an hour for the dough to proof while you prepare your oven.
2. Place a stone, steel, or baking sheet on the middle shelf of your oven. If you have a big roasting pan, place it over your dough and stone for steam. If not, place an aluminum pan with a pinhole in it on the oven shelf below the stone. This makes way for steam to drip. When making the pinhole, make sure it drips about 1-2 drops per second over your sink.
3. Set your oven to 500°F and let it heat up for 30 minutes.
4. On an upside-down or rimless baking sheet, place a sheet of parchment paper.
5. If you're doing the drip pan, boil a cup of water in the microwave when the oven is hot, and the final proof is done.
6. Take the birotes and place them on the parchment paper. Score them down the middle and at an angle of about 60°. (rather than 90°).
7. Transfer the parchment paper onto the heated stone. Right away, pour the boiling cup of water onto the aluminum pan below or put the upside-down roasting pan on top of the dough. Then, shut the oven door to keep the steam inside.
8. Bake at 500°F for 10 minutes (if using, place the roasting pan on top of the dough).
9. Reduce the oven temperature to 475°F (remove the roasting pan) and bake for about 10 minutes more. If you want an even browning, turn the baguettes.
10. For an extra 10 minutes, turn off the oven and prop the door open with the wooden spoon.
11. The birotes can be left out for 1-2 days before wrapping them to keep them from hardening, and they can be toasted before eating to re-crisp the crust. Once they are fully cooled, you can also wrap and bag them to freeze.

3. Bolillo (White Bread)

Prep Time: 30 Minutes / Cook Time: 30 Minutes / Rising Time: 90 Minutes / Total Time: 2 Hours 30 Minutes / Yield: 10 loaves

Ingredients
- 4 cups bread flour
- 1 1/3 cups warm water
- 1 large egg white, beaten
- 1 (1/4-ounce) packet of active dry yeast
- 1 teaspoon sugar
- 1 teaspoon salt

Instructions
1. Get the ingredients together.
2. Add water to the large mixing bowl and sprinkle yeast on the surface.
3. Now, mix the sugar, salt, and flour in a different bowl.
4. Mix in the water a little at a time and the flour mixture until a dough forms. Add more flour, one tablespoon at a time, until a stiff dough forms if this flour-to-water ratio is insufficient to create a cohesive dough.
5. After putting the dough in a greased bowl and covering it with a towel or cloth, let it rise for about an hour in a warm location.
6. Next, remove the dough from the bowl, punch it down, and knead it for about 10 minutes on a lightly floured surface until smooth.
7. Make 10 balls out of the dough.
8. Roll the balls between your palms for around five seconds to form a cylindrical shape that tapers slightly at the ends if you want to make oval-shaped rolls. Place the pieces on one or more baking sheets. Cover with a towel and keep the loaves to rise for another 30 minutes.
9. Warm the oven up to 375 F. Use egg white to cover each dough ball. Score the top of each roll longways, about 1/4 inch deep.
10. Bake the loaves for about thirty minutes or until they are cooked through and browned. Take it out of the oven. Allow it to cool fully or just a little, then eat it warm.

4. Cemitas (Mexican Sesame Seed Sandwich Buns)

Prep Time: 15 Minutes / Cook Time: 15 Minutes / Rising Time: 5 Hours / Total Time: 5 Hours 30 Minutes / Yield: 6 buns

Ingredients
- 12.5 oz (2 1/2 cups) all-purpose flour
- 8 ounces heavy cream
- Coarse sea salt
- 3 eggs, divided
- 1 teaspoon instant yeast
- 1/2 cup sesame seeds
- 3 tablespoons sugar
- 1 1/2 tsp of kosher salt (or 3/4 teaspoons of table salt)

Instructions
1. In a food processor bowl, combine flour, cream, sugar, yeast, and two eggs. Continue until a ball of dough that rides around the blade is formed, around 45 seconds. It will be a very sticky dough. Or, use the stand mixer with a paddle attachment to form a dough; simply add ingredients and mix on medium speed until a homogenous dough comes together.
2. After transferring the dough to a sizable mixing bowl and securely covering it with plastic wrap, allow it to rise at room temperature for approximately four hours or until it has doubled in size.
3. Transfer the dough to a work surface that has been lightly floured. Form it into a big ball, then cut it into six equal pieces with the sharp knife or bench scraper. Now, shape each piece into a ball using your lightly floured hands. Place the dough balls on the rimmed baking sheet covered with parchment, tucking the seam under. After covering it with plastic wrap that has been weighted down with a kitchen towel, leave it at room temperature for an hour.
4. Meanwhile, preheat the oven to 450°F (230°C) and center the oven rack. Once ready to bake, combine the remaining egg and 1 tablespoon of water. Using a brush, evenly coat each bun with the egg mixture. Next, add a generous amount of sesame seeds and a small pinch of coarse salt. Bake for 12 to 15 minutes or until deeply golden brown. Take the buns out of the oven, place them on a wire cooling rack, and allow them to cool completely before using.

5. Bolillos (Crusty Mexican Bread Rolls)

Prep Time: 25 Minutes / Cook Time: 25-30 Minutes / Resting Time: 2-3 Hours / Total Time: 4 Hours / Yield: 9-10 rolls

Ingredients:

- 1 extra large egg white beaten with 1 tsp. water
- 1 1/2 tsp. salt
- 1 1/3 cups warm water
- 1 Tbsp. honey (prefer Sue Bee's honey)
- 1 packet of fast-rising active dry yeast or 2 1/4 tsp of active dry yeast
- 3 1/4 - 4 cups flour
- 1 Tbsp. butter melted

Instructions:

1. Put the yeast in a large bowl with warm water. Stir it in, then let it sit for 5 minutes.
2. Once the yeast begins to foam, mix the honey, melted butter, and salt. Allow it to work for another 5–10 minutes.
3. Include 2 1/2 cups of flour and mix. Mix on low speed to combine; next, beat on medium speed for around 5 minutes or until the dough is very stretchy.
4. Add as much of the remaining flour as necessary gradually to form a soft dough. (Because it's so cold and dry here right now, I only added 1/8 cup more after the 3 1/4 cups.)
5. Work the dough on a lightly floured surface until it becomes smooth and elastic, about 15 to 20 minutes. Alternatively, use the dough hook on your mixer and "knead" the dough for 8–10 minutes.
6. Fill a large bowl with about 1 teaspoon of oil, and use your hands to coat the entire interior. Place the dough ball in the bowl and turn it so that all of its sides have an oily sheen. (If you need to, add a little more oil.)
7. It will take about two to three hours to rise in a warm place with the lid on. (I turn on the oven light and put the dough in it to rise.)
8. It takes three hours for mine to double.
9. Push down the dough and knead lightly on a lightly floured surface. The dough should be a little sticky.
10. Make 8–10 balls out of the dough. Roll it out into ovals using the palms of your hands.
11. Each piece should be between 4 and 5 inches long, tapering to each end at 1 1/2 to 2 inches in the middle (or as desired).
12. Place the rolls on a parchment-lined and sprayed baking sheet, cover them with lightly sprayed plastic wrap, and allow to rise until doubled about 1 hour.
13. In the meantime, preheat the oven to 375°F. (Let rolls rise in another warm spot or in an off-the-shelf secondary oven with the light on.)
14. Beat the egg white with the water until frothy, then baste the rolls thoroughly.
15. Make a cut in the middle of each roll, stopping about 1/2" from each end and going about 1/2" deep.
16. Bake for 25 to 30 minutes or until rolls are browned and hollow when tapped. Take them off the baking sheets and put them on racks to cool.
17. At last, serve it hot and fresh from the oven.

6. Bunuelos (Mexican Fritters)

Prep Time: 45 Minutes / Cook Time: 10 Minutes / Total Time: 55 Minutes / Yield: 8 bunuelos

Ingredients:

For the Bunuelos:

- 4 tablespoons of oil, plus 2 or more cups for frying
- 1 1/2 teaspoon baking powder
- 3/4 cup warm water
- 2 cups all-purpose flour
- 1/2 teaspoon salt

For the cinnamon sugar topping:

- 1 tablespoon ground cinnamon
- 1/2 cup granulated sugar

Instructions:

For the Bunuelos:

1. In the large bowl, mix together salt, baking powder, and all-purpose flour. Stir until well combined.
2. Stir in 4 tablespoons of oil and warm water. Using a spoon or your hands, combine until the dough comes together.
3. After transferring the dough to a clean surface, knead it for eight to ten minutes or until it becomes elastic and smooth.
4. Form the dough into a ball, transfer it to a bowl, warp it with a kitchen towel, and set it aside to rest for half an hour.
5. Fill a large sauté pan with one to two inches of frying oil, cover a large plate with paper towels, and prepare the cinnamon sugar topping while the dough is resting. Put aside.
6. Now, cut the dough into 8 equal parts and roll each into a ball. Roll each ball out into an 8 to 10-inch circle on a lightly floured surface; use a floured rolling pin. (It is best to arrange the rolled-out dough in a single layer on a large kitchen towel. The rolled-out dough may stick if you stack it on top of each other.)
7. Preheat 350°F in the frying oil. Fry each circle of dough for about 60 seconds, turning once or until both sides are golden brown. Move to a plate that has been prepared to remove any extra oil. Next, sprinkle with a generous amount of cinnamon sugar topping.

To make the cinnamon sugar topping:

1. In a small bowl, mix ground cinnamon and granulated sugar.

7. Calabacitas Cornbread (Zucchini Cornbread)

Prep Time: 20 Minutes / Cook Time: 50 Minutes / Total Time: 1Hour 10 Minutes / Yield: 8

Ingredients

Bowl 1:

- 1 cup grated zucchini or any summer squash
- ½ – ¾ cup chopped roasted Chile (or both)
- 1 cup corn (corn from 1 cob)
- 2 scallions, minced (white and green parts)
- 1 cup grated cheese, cheddar, Monterey Jack or both

Bowl 2:

- ½ cup flour
- 1 ½ tsp. baking powder
- ½ tsp. salt
- 1 cup finely ground cornmeal

Bowl 3:

- ¾ cup milk
- 2 Tbsp. melted butter
- 2 eggs
- ½ cup yogurt

Instructions

1. Preheat oven to 350º F.
2. Apply butter or cooking oil spray to a 1- to 2-quart casserole dish. Put aside.
3. Bowl 1: Fill the bowl with the cheese and vegetables, stirring to combine them evenly.
4. In bowl 2: whisk together flour, baking powder, salt, and cornmeal.
5. In bowl 3: whisk together the milk, yogurt, butter, and eggs.
6. Combine Bowl 1 (vegetables) and Bowl 2 (cornmeal mixture). Stir to mix the cornmeal mixture into the vegetables with a spatula.
7. Transfer the egg mixture (Bowl 3) to the mixture of vegetable cornmeal. Gently stir all the ingredients together. Once mixed, do not stir anymore. Make sure not to overmix and destroy the baking powder.
8. Pour into the prepared casserole dish.
9. Bake for 40 to 60 minutes, or until thoroughly cooked, in a preheated oven. (Put a toothpick in the center to check for doneness. It's finished if it comes out clean. If not, continue cooking for another 5 minutes and retest.)
10. Take it out of the oven and allow it to rest for five minutes before slicing.

8. Capirotada (Mexican Bread Pudding)

Prep Time: 10 Minutes / Cook Time: 50 Minutes / Total Time: 1 Hour / Yield: 10

Ingredients

- 3 large bananas, sliced into rounds
- 2 cups of shredded Oaxaca cheese (or use any melty white cheese like Monterey Jack, Provolone or Mozzarella)
- 5 cups nonfat milk
- 3 cinnamon sticks
- 1 cup raisins
- oil or butter for greasing
- 1/2 cup sliced almonds
- 2 whole cloves
- 4 large bolillo bread rolls, cut into 1-inch-thick pieces (about 10–12 cups)
- 1 (8-ounce) cone piloncillo (or use 1 1/4 cup dark brown sugar)

Instructions

1. Set the oven temperature to 350°F. Grease a 913-inch baking dish (or a slightly larger dish) with oil or butter. Put aside.
2. Put the cubed bolillo bread on a large baking sheet. Bake for about 5 minutes or until the bread is slightly toasted and dried out. Take it out of the oven and put it aside.
3. Add the milk, piloncillo, cinnamon sticks, and cloves to a large pot over medium-high heat. After whisking everything together, gently boil it.
4. Turn down the heat to low and simmer, covered, for ten minutes, whisking now and then. Take it off the burner and throw away the cloves and cinnamon sticks.
5. Assemble the capirotada by putting half of the toasted bread in the baking dish in a single layer. Place half of the raisins, half of the sliced almonds, half of the shredded cheese, and all of the banana slices on top. Repeat the process with the remaining ingredients to create one more layer.
6. Pour the sweetened milk evenly over the capirotada, paying special attention to the bread on the edges.
7. Put aluminum foil over the dish and bake it for another 15 minutes. Then, take off the foil and bake it for another 15 minutes without it.
8. Take it out of the oven, give it five minutes to cool, then serve it warm. Alternately, let it cool fully, cover it, place it in the refrigerator, and serve it cold.

9. Cemita Rolls (Sandwich)

Prep Time: 45 Minutes / Cook Time: 20 Minutes / Inactive Time: 6 Hours / Total Time: 7 Hours 5 Minutes / Yield: 8 rolls

Ingredients

- 567 grams (20 ounces) unbleached all-purpose flour, divided
- 2 teaspoons of sugar
- 12 ounces water at 100 degrees F
- 1 1/2 teaspoons salt
- 1 large egg
- 1 1/2 teaspoons instant yeast
- 2 tablespoons lard, butter, or shortening
- Sesame seeds for topping

Instructions

1. Fill the stand mixer's bowl with the water, yeast, sugar, lard, and 312 grams (11 ounces) of flour. Add the egg and use the whisk attachment to mix on medium for five minutes.
2. Next, switch to the dough hook and add 6 more ounces of flour. Mix on low for around 5 minutes.
3. Add flour by the tablespoon while mixing on low until you have a soft dough that is tacky but not sticky. Almost all of the remaining flour was used. Stir for five more minutes.
4. Put the dough into the greased bowl, wrap it with plastic wrap, and let it rise for three to four hours, or until doubled, in a cool place (65 degrees F).
5. Deflated the dough, covered the container with plastic wrap, and allowed it to rise in a cool place for a further three hours or more until it had doubled.
6. Form the dough into 8 equal pieces and roll into small balls. Move them to a baking sheet that has been lined with parchment or oil, then cover with oiled plastic wrap. Allow it to sit for 30 minutes.
7. After 30 minutes, gently press the balls down with your fingers to flatten to a thickness of one inch. Once more, wrap the rolls in plastic wrap. Let it rise for an additional 30 minutes.
8. Place a baking stone on the center rack and preheat the oven to 450 degrees Fahrenheit. If you don't have a baking stone, a baking sheet will suffice. (Preheating the baking sheet is not necessary.)
9. Drizzle the rolls with water and top with sesame seeds.
10. Bake the rolls until golden brown, around 20 minutes. On a wire rack, cool.

10. Conchas (Mexican Sweet Bread)

Prep Time: 20 Minutes / Cook Time: 20 Minutes / Additional Time: 1 Hours 45 / Total Time: 2 Hours 25 Minutes / Yield: 12 conchas

Ingredients
Bread:

- ⅜ cup white sugar
- ⅓ cup butter, melted
- ½ teaspoon ground cinnamon
- 1 large egg
- ½ cup evaporated milk
- ½ cup warm water
- 1 teaspoon salt
- 2 ½ teaspoons yeast
- 4 cups all-purpose flour

Topping:

- 1 cup all-purpose flour
- ½ cup butter softened
- ⅔ cup white sugar
- 2 teaspoons ground cinnamon
- 1 teaspoon vanilla extract

Instructions

1. Gather all of the ingredients.
2. To prepare the bread: In a large bowl, mix yeast with warm water. Then, let it sit for about 5 minutes or until the yeast softens and starts to form a creamy foam.
3. Add the milk, sugar, egg, salt, and 2 cups of flour. Mix until everything is well mixed.
4. Add cinnamon and the remaining 2 cups flour gradually until the dough comes together.
5. Then, turn the dough out onto the floured surface and knead for about 6-8 minutes or until smooth and elastic. Transfer to a large, well-greased bowl and turn to coat the dough.
6. Cover and let rise for about one hour, or until doubled, in a warm location.
7. In the meantime, make the topping: Using an electric mixer, mix butter and sugar in a medium-sized bowl until the mixture is light and fluffy.
8. Blend in the flour until a thick paste forms.
9. Move half of the paste to a different bowl. Combine cinnamon and vanilla in one-half of the mixture.
10. Cut the dough into 12 equal pieces. Roll into balls, then put on a cookie sheet that has been oiled three inches apart.
11. Separate each topping bowl into 6 balls and pat flat. Put circles of topping on top of the dough balls and lightly press them down. Cut seashell-like grooves in the topping with a knife.
12. Let it rise for about 45 minutes with the lid on.
13. Warm the oven up to 190 degrees C (375 degrees F).
14. It will take about 20 minutes of baking in a hot oven until it turns a light golden-brown color.

11. Corn Tortillas

Prep Time: 25 Minutes / Cook Time: 20 Minutes / Total Time: 45 Minutes / Yield: 15 Tortillas

Ingredients

- 1 teaspoon fine sea salt
- 1 1/2-2 cups of hot water
- 2 cups (240 grams) masa harina

Instructions

1. Mix the dough: In the large mixing bowl, whisk together masa harina and salt. Add 1 1/2 cups hot water gradually, stirring with a silicone spatula or use wooden spoon until an evenly mixed dough forms. Knead the dough in the bowl with your hands for two to three minutes, until it is smooth and comes together into a ball. The texture of the dough should be firm and springy, like Play-Doh. If the dough is too wet and sticks to your hands, add a few tablespoons more flour. Add one or two more tablespoons of hot water if it feels too dry and crackly.
2. Rest the dough: Allow the dough to rest for around 10 minutes after covering it with a damp kitchen towel (or paper towel).
3. Portion the dough: To make a 2-tablespoon ball (around the size of a golf ball or 35-40 grams), portion the dough with a spoon or a medium ice cream scoop, then roll the ball with your hands until it is nice and round.
4. Press the dough balls: In a tortilla push, put the dough ball between two pieces of plastic wrap. Then, press the dough ball gently until it turns into a 4- to 5-inch tortilla.
5. To make the tortilla: Set a comal or nonstick skillet over medium-high heat. Once the pan is hot, carefully take the tortilla out of the plastic wrap and lay it flat in the pan. Cook the tortilla for 40 to 60 seconds on each side, flipping it over when the bottom starts to get brown spots. The tortillas will most likely bubble up as they cook, especially on the second side, which is a good sign! Once cooked, place the tortilla in a tortilla warmer or the bowl wrapped in a clean kitchen towel to keep it from drying out.
6. Repeat with the remaining tortillas: To continue the cycle, I suggest pressing the next dough ball and cooking one tortilla at a time. Adjust the heat a little bit if you think the skillet is getting too hot.
7. Serve: As they sit in a stack in the tortilla warmer (or wrapped in a towel), the tortillas will continue to soften a little bit more. So, I recommend starting with the tortillas at the bottom of the stack, as they will be the softest. Enjoy, and serve however you wish!

12. Galletas de Suero (Buttermilk Biscuits)

Prep Time: 5 Minutes / Cook Time: 22 Minutes / Total Time: 27 Minutes / Yield: 1 dozen biscuits

Ingredients

- 1 1/2 teaspoons baking powder
- 2 cups (or more) Suero (whey) or use buttermilk (used as a substitute)
- 4 cups (or more) all-purpose flour
- 1/3 cup Crisco

Instructions

1. Warm the oven up to 350°F.
2. Put the flour and baking powder in a large bowl and mix them together. Add the Crisco and cut it in until it's well mixed. Now, create a well in the middle of the mixture and add the Suero slowly. Using your fingers, knead the dough, adding Suero as needed. It's fine if the dough is sticky; more flour can be added if necessary. But I like it a little sticky. The galletas will be less sticky.
3. After kneading the dough until it is smooth on a work surface, divide it into 12 to 14 balls. Pat out until around one inch thick.
4. Use a fork to poke each ball twice. Place on the ungreased baking sheet and bake for 20 to 23 minutes. One more minute under the broiler or until golden brown.

13. Elotes Pan de Dulce (Mexican Corn Sweet Bread)

Prep Time: 45 Minutes / Cook Time: 20 Minutes / Resting Time: 1 Hours / Total Time: 2 Hours 5 Minutes / Yield: 15 Elotes

Ingredients

For Dough:

- 1/2 cup shortening
- 1/3 cup sugar
- 1 teaspoon active dry yeast
- 1/2 teaspoon salt
- 1 large egg, slightly beaten
- 2 cups flour
- 1/4 cup warm water
- 1 teaspoon cinnamon
- 1/2 teaspoon ground anise, optional

For Filling:

- 1/2 cup powdered sugar
- 1/2 cup softened butter
- 1 egg yolk
- 2/3 cup flour
- 1/2 teaspoon cinnamon
- more sugar for dusting
- Zest of 1 orange optional
- 2 drops of yellow food coloring optional

Instructions

1. Put the two cups of flour on a flat surface or a big cutting board. Add 1 teaspoon of yeast, 1/2 teaspoon of salt, and 1/3 cup of sugar to the flour. Use your hands to mix the ingredients together. Add the egg and mix it in with your fingers. Add the water slowly; the dough will be lumpy. Mix in the cinnamon, anise, and shortening. For about 5 to 7 minutes, knead the dough until it is smooth. Set it aside for 30 minutes with the lid on.
2. Warm the oven up to 375 degrees F. Next, place parchment paper on the baking sheet and set it aside.
3. Mix all filling ingredients together in the separate bowl. Use your hands to mix until dough forms. Create 15 small balls and roll them between your palms to form a skinny cigar shape, about 2 inches long. Place on a plate, cover, and set aside.
4. Create 15 equal dough balls with the reserved dough. With wax paper on the inside of a tortilla press, press the dough ball out to about 3 inches. Cut straight lines across the flattened dough with a knife or metal spatula. After turning it over, score it again so it goes over the other lines.
5. Carefully turn it over and add the filling down the middle. Fold the sides in and press to seal. Pinch the end together and form it into the shape of an ear of corn.
6. Put to a lined baking sheet, seam side down. Put some sugar on it. Set it aside for 30 minutes with the lid on. Put the pan in the hot oven and bake for 20 minutes, turning it over halfway through. Bake until it turns golden. Let it cool completely before putting it in a container that won't let air in.

14. Mantecadas (Mexican Muffins)

Prep Time: 25 Minutes / Cook Time: 20 Minutes / Total Time: 45 Minutes / Yield: 12 mantecadas

Ingredients:

- 1 tablespoon baking powder
- 1 tablespoon orange zest
- ⅛ teaspoon salt
- 2 teaspoons Mexican vanilla extract
- ½ cup light olive oil
- 3 large eggs at room temperature
- ½ teaspoon baking soda
- 1 ¾ cups all-purpose flour
- 5 tablespoons cornstarch
- ½ cup granulated sugar
- ½ cup milk

Instructions:

1. Warm the oven up to 400 F. Use red cupcake liners to line a muffin pan with 12 holes.
2. Now, on medium-high speed, mix the sugar and eggs until the mixture is foamy and pale yellow. Add the vanilla and beat again.
3. Put the oil and half of the milk into a small jug with a lid. Slowly pour the milk and oil into the egg mixture. Mix on medium-high speed until all the liquid is mixed in.
4. In the different bowl, sift together the dry ingredients (baking soda, cornstarch, flour, baking powder, and salt). Mix them in the egg mixture again by sifting them, and beat on medium speed until everything is well mixed.
5. Mix on medium-high speed after adding the rest of the milk until the batter is very smooth and lump-free.
6. Fill each cup three-quarters full with batter after pouring it into a jug with a spout.
7. Lower the oven temperature to 350 F right before putting the muffins in. Bake for 20 minutes or until a toothpick stuck in the middle comes out clean.
8. Take them out of the muffin pan and allow them to chill down on the wire rack for a minimum of fifteen minutes before serving.

15. Marranitos (Mexican Gingerbread Pigs)

Prep Time: 20 Minutes / Cook Time: 10-12 Minutes / Total Time: 30 Minutes / Yield: 28 cookies

Ingredients:

- 1 ½ teaspoons baking soda
- ¼ cup milk
- 2 tsp ground ginger
- 1 ½ teaspoons vanilla extract
- ¾ cup unsulfured molasses
- 1 ½ teaspoons ground cinnamon
- 2 large eggs
- 1 cup dark brown sugar, packed
- ½ cup unsalted butter, softened (about 1 stick)
- 5 cups all-purpose flour

Instructions:

1. Warm the oven up to 350°F. Put parchment paper on cookie sheets and set them aside.
2. Put butter in the stand mixer's bowl and mix it in until it's smooth. Mix in the dark brown sugar until it's well mixed in. Add the milk, vanilla extract, molasses, and one egg. Combine and blend until smooth.
3. Put the cinnamon, ground ginger, baking soda, and flour in a separate large bowl. Mix everything together.
4. Next, combine the dry ingredients into the wet ingredients one cup at a time until everything is well mixed. The dough should easily be pulled away from the mixing bowl.
5. Roll out the dough to a thickness of 3/8 inch (or slightly less than 1/2 inch) on a lightly floured surface. To make pig shapes, use a cookie cutter like this one. On the prepared baking sheets, place the pigs 1 1/2 inches apart. Brush the tops of the cookies with the remaining beaten egg.
6. Crack the remaining egg into the small bowl and whisk it in. Using the pastry brush, cover the tops of the pigs with the beaten egg.
7. Put it in the oven for 10 to 12 minutes or until the edges start to brown a little.

16. Mexican Cheese Bread

Prep Time: 10 Minutes / Cook Time: 20 Minutes / Total Time: 30 Minutes / Yield: 20 slices

Ingredients

- 2 tsp. taco seasoning or to taste
- 1/2 cup mayonnaise
- 1/2 cup of diced red or green bell pepper, seeds, and membranes removed or more as desired
- 1/2 cup unsalted butter, very softened
- 1 loaf of crusty French or Italian bread
- 1 cup shredded cheddar or Colby-jack cheese

Instructions

1. Warm the oven up to 325 degrees. Arrange a large-rimmed baking sheet with a sheet of foil or parchment paper on top.
2. Mix the butter, mayonnaise, and taco seasoning together in a medium-sized bowl. Set this aside.
3. Slice the loaf of bread in 1/2 lengthwise with a serrated knife; place the bread halves cut-side-up on a baking sheet.
4. Now, spread the prepared butter mixture over the bread, dividing it evenly between the loaves with your favorite spreader or a skinny spatula. After sprinkling the cheese over each loaf, arrange the desired number of diced bell peppers on top.
5. Next, put the bread on the middle rack of the oven, uncovered, and bake for 20-25 minutes, or until it is hot all the way through and bubbly on top.
6. Cut each loaf of cheese bread into 10 slices, or as many as you'd like, using your favorite pizza cutter. Serve right away.

17. Mexican Chocolate Banana Bread

Prep Time: 5 Minutes / Cook Time: 1 Hours / Total Time: 1 Hours 5 Minutes / Yield: 8

Ingredients

- 1 1/4 cups of all-purpose flour, plus more for pan
- 1/2 cup unsalted butter, divided (1 stick)
- 1/2 teaspoon ground cinnamon
- 1 large egg
- 1/4 teaspoon salt
- 1 teaspoon pure vanilla extract
- 1 teaspoon baking soda
- 2 tablespoons unsweetened cocoa powder
- ¼ cup crema Mexicana, or sour cream
- 3/4 cup granulated sugar
- ¼ cup chopped pecan or walnuts
- 4 very ripe bananas
- 1 (3.3 ounces) tablet Mexican chocolate, grated

Instructions

1. First, warm the oven up to 350 degrees F.
2. Use one tbsp. of butter to grease a 9x5-inch loaf pan. Next, sprinkle flour over the pan and tap out any extra.
3. Peel and mash ripe bananas with a potato masher until smooth.
4. When the butter is melted, add it to the mashed bananas.
5. Add the beaten egg, vanilla extract, sugar, salt, and crema and mix them in.
6. In a different bowl, combine the baking soda, ground cinnamon, cocoa powder, grated chocolate, and flour very quickly with a whisk.
7. Mix the flour and salt together with the banana mixture. Make sure the flour is just mixed in, and then add the pecans.
8. Place the batter in the pan that has been prepared, and use the spatula to smooth the top.
9. Bake, rotating halfway through, until the batter is set and the sides are beginning to pull away from the pan, and a toothpick inserted into the center of the bread comes out clean, 60 to 65 minutes.
10. Let it cool for at least 15 minutes in the pan on a wire rack.
11. Run a butter knife around the outside of the pan to loosen the loaf. Then, gently tap the pan on its side until the loaf comes out. Move to a plate or cutting board and let it cool completely before cutting.

18. Mexican Chocolate Zucchini Bread

Prep Time: 10 Minutes / Cook Time: 50 Minutes / Total Time: 1 Hours / Yield: 16

Ingredients

- 2 teaspoons vanilla extract
- 1/2 teaspoon kosher salt
- 2 eggs, beaten
- 3.3-ounce Mexican chocolate tablet, shredded into a powder
- 2 large zucchinis, shredded, 3 ½-4 cups grated
- 3 cups all-purpose flour
- 2 teaspoons of baking soda
- 3/4 cup granulated sugar
- 2 teaspoons of butter or shortening for greasing the pans
- ½ cup unsalted butter, melted
- 2 teaspoons ground cinnamon

Instructions

1. First, warm the oven up to 350 degrees F.
2. Put the grated zucchini in the colander set over a bowl to drain off any extra moisture.
3. Grease two 5 x 9-inch loaf pans.
4. Mix the baking soda, flour, and ground cinnamon together in a large bowl using a whisk.
5. Mix the sugar, eggs, vanilla, and salt in a different bowl using a whisk. Now add the chocolate, zucchini, and melted butter and mix them in.
6. Mix the flour mixture into the sugar egg zucchini mixture until well combined.
7. Now, grease 2 loaf pans and divide the batter equally between them.
8. Bake for 45 to 50 minutes or until a toothpick stuck in the middle comes out clean.
9. Allow pans to cool for 10 minutes before removing to a wire rack to cool.

19. Mexican Corn Bread

Prep Time: 15 Minutes / Cook Time: 45 Minutes / Total Time: 1 Hours / Yield: 1 pan cornbread

Ingredients

- 5 large eggs
- 1 tablespoon baking soda
- 2 ½ cups cornmeal
- 2 teaspoons vanilla extract
- ½ cup all-purpose flour
- 1 (15-ounce) can cream-style corn
- 2 (15.25 oz) cans whole kernel corn, drained and rinsed
- ½ cup butter, melted
- 1 teaspoon salt
- 1 (14 oz) can sweetened condensed milk (as La Lechera)
- ½ cup white sugar (Optional)

Instructions

1. First, turn the oven on to 350 degrees F (175 degrees C). Grease and flour a 2-quart baking dish.
2. In a large bowl, mix sugar and sweetened condensed milk with a whisk. Add eggs and vanilla and mix well. Combine butter, cream-style corn, whole kernel corn, and mix them together.
3. In a different bowl, mix the cornmeal, baking soda, flour, and salt together using a whisk. Then, add the cornmeal mixture to the corn mixture and stir it in.
4. Put batter into the baking dish that has been prepared.
5. It takes about 45 minutes of baking until a toothpick stuck in the middle of the cornbread comes out clean. Warm up and serve.

20. Mexican Corn Muffin Mix bread

Prep Time: 5 Minutes / Cook Time: 35 Minutes / Total Time: 40 Minutes / Yield: 15

Ingredients

- 14.75-ounce can cream-style corn
- 3 tablespoons vegetable oil
- ½ cup of sour cream (light or regular) or plain Greek yogurt
- ½ cup of frozen yellow corn; no need to thaw
- 1 cup of shredded Monterey Jack or pepper Jack cheese
- 3 large eggs
- 4-ounce can of diced green chiles, drained
- 17 ounces Jiffy Corn Muffin Mix (two 8.5-ounce packages)

Instructions

1. Use nonstick cooking spray to coat a 13 x 9-inch baking dish. Now, warm the oven up to 375 degrees F.
2. With a wooden spoon, mix the eggs and oil together well. Put in the sour cream, cheese, diced green chiles, creamed corn, and frozen corn. Mix everything together well. Mix in the Jiffy Corn Muffin Mix until it's just barely moist. The batter will be lumpy.
3. Put the mixture into the baking dish that has been prepared. Bake for 30 to 35 minutes, or until a toothpick stuck in the middle comes out clean.

21. Mexican Fry Bread (Mexican Fried Gorditas)

Prep Time: 15 Minutes / Cook Time: 5 Minutes / Total Time: 20 Minutes / Yield: 6

Ingredients

- 4 tablespoons vegetable shortening
- 1/4 teaspoon salt
- 1 1/2 tablespoons baking powder
- 2 cups all-purpose flour
- 1/4 cup oil (for frying)
- 2/3 cup of water or 2/3 cup milk

Instructions

1. Mix together flour, baking powder, salt, and shortening until the shortening is well combined. Add water and mix well.
2. Take the dough out onto the lightly floured board; knead for 2 minutes or until smooth.
3. Make a ball out of the dough and put it in a plastic bag.
4. Separate the dough and roll it out to make six 4- to 6-inch thin, flat rounds.
5. Heat the oil to 375 degrees F in a cast iron pan.
6. Put the rounds in the oil and cook for 20-30 seconds on each side, until they are light golden brown.
7. Remove the rounds from the skillet using a slotted spoon, then drain on paper towels.
8. Fill as desired with prepared fillings.

22. Mexican Garlic Cheese Bread

Prep Time: 15 Minutes / Cook Time: 20 Minutes / Total Time: 35 Minutes / Yield: 6

Ingredients

- 1 4 ounce can chop, black, olives
- 2 tbsp finely chopped onion or 2 tsp granulated onion
- 1 cup mayonnaise
- 1 loaf French Bread
- 1/4 cup melted butter
- 4 tbsp chopped jalapenos
- 1/2 tsp granulated garlic
- 13 ounces grated cheddar cheese

Instructions

1. First, split a loaf of French bread in half lengthwise. Warm the oven up to 350 degrees.
2. Put the melted butter, chopped olives, green onion, jalapenos, and spices in a large bowl. Mix the ingredients together. After these are well mixed together, add the grated cheese.
3. Next, split the cheese mixture in half and evenly distribute each half over the French bread.
4. After preheating the oven, put the cheese bread inside and bake it for about 20 minutes or until it becomes bubbly.
5. After letting it cool for 5 to 10 minutes, use a large knife to cut it into 2-inch pieces. Enjoy.

23. Mexican Monkey Bread

Prep Time: 10 Minutes / Cook Time: 40 Minutes /
Additional Time: 5 Minutes / Total Time: 55 Minutes /
Yield: 1 loaf

Ingredients

- ¾ cup jalapeno pepper slices, divided
- ¼ cup shredded mozzarella cheese
- 2 tablespoons butter, melted
- cooking spray
- ¾ teaspoon dried parsley flakes, divided
- 1 (16.3 ounces) package of refrigerated buttermilk biscuit dough, separated and each portion cut into quarters
- 1 ¼ cups shredded Cheddar cheese, divided

Instructions

1. First, set the oven temperature to 350 F (175 C). Use cooking spray to prepare a 9x5-inch loaf pan.
2. In a small bowl, melt the butter. Coat each piece of biscuit dough in melted butter.
3. Place enough biscuit dough pieces in the loaf pans bottom to create a single layer, then sprinkle 1/4 cup pepper slices, 1/2 cup Cheddar cheese, and 1/4 teaspoon parsley on top. After one more layering, add the remaining biscuit dough pieces, pepper slices, and parsley flakes on top.
4. In the bowl, combine the remaining 1/4 cup Cheddar cheese and mozzarella cheese; spread over the top of the ingredients to cover.
5. In a hot oven, bake for 40 to 45 minutes or until golden brown. Allow the bread to chill in the pan for around 5 minutes before inverting onto a plate to serve.

24. Mexican Niño Envuelto (Mexican Jelly Roll)

Prep Time: 15 Minutes / Cook Time: 8 Minutes / Total Time: 30-35 Minutes / Yield: 8

Ingredients:

- 2/3 cups flour 75 gr, shifted
- 1 teaspoon vanilla extract
- 1/4 cup unsweetened coconut
- 1/3 heaping cup of sugar 75 gr + 1/2 teaspoon
- A little bit of softened butter or use canola oil (to grease the baking sheet)
- 3 medium-sized eggs approx. 130 gr / 4.6 oz, room temperature
- 1 teaspoon baking powder
- 1/3 cup strawberry marmalade

Instructions:

1. First, set the oven to 400 °F (200 °C) before you start.
2. Now, cover the baking sheet with parchment paper and grease it with butter. Press the paper against the sheet's edges and all the way around it. Make an extra sheet of parchment paper for later rolling the cake.
3. Mix the sugar and egg on high speed until fluffy and airy. The mixture will turn a light beige color, and the beaters of the mixer will leave marks on it. It will take about four to five minutes.
4. Mix in vanilla for an additional few second. Take out the mixer.
5. Add the baking powder and sifted flour to the egg-sugar mixture.
6. Use the spatula to fold the flour into the liquid ingredients carefully. Be careful not to over-mix the sponge because we want it to stay light.
7. Put the batter onto the prepared baking sheet and spread it evenly with the spatula, ensuring it covers all four corners.
8. Bake for 8 minutes, but don't overbake; start checking at 7 minutes with a toothpick inserted into the center. It's ready if it comes out clean.
9. After taking the sponge out of the oven, give it a minute or two to cool down. It is critical to roll the sponge while it is warm; otherwise, it will break. So, you want to start rolling it as soon as you can without getting burned.
10. Put a little sugar on top of the sponge, then put the other parchment sheet (or kitchen towel) on top of it. To remove the sponge, turn the baking sheet over quickly and carefully.
11. Remove the parchment paper from the sponge's top. Take one end of the bottom piece of parchment paper and roll it up. Don't worry about the paper in the middle.
12. Allow it to cool for another 3 minutes. In the meantime, stir the strawberry marmalade until it becomes spreadable. If it's too thick, add 1/8 teaspoon of water at a time.
13. After unrolling the sponge, use half of the strawberry marmalade to spread a thin layer across the surface.
14. Roll it once more, this time peeling the paper back as you go. Ensure that the seam of the sponge is at the base.
15. Cover with the remaining strawberry marmalade and coconut.

25. Mexican Semita Bread (Semitas Chorreadas)

Prep Time: 15 Minutes / Cook Time: 20 Minutes / Resting Time: 1 Hour 20 Minutes / Total Time: 1 Hour 55 Minutes / Yield: 4

Ingredients:

- 1 tsp. Active dry yeast
- ½ cup of Chopped pecans
- ½ cup of Raisins, soaked in the juice of one orange
- 1 tsp. Ground anise seed
- 1 ½ cups Warm water
- ½ cup Dark brown sugar
- 1 tsp. orange zest
- 3.5 oz Piloncillo (about ½ cup)
- ⅓ cup Coconut butter, about 3 oz
- 1 tsp Freshly ground cinnamon (Ceylon)
- 3 ½ cup Bread flour
- ½ tsp. Salt

Instructions:

1. Add the flour, sugar, anise, cinnamon, yeast, and salt to a large bowl. Mix them all together.
2. Stir in the coconut butter and warm water, then knead.
3. Mix the dough for four to six minutes at medium-low speed with the hook attachment on my mixer or until it is stretchy but not sticky and has come away from the sides of the bowl.
4. If you don't have a mixer, knead by hand for 10 minutes or until the desired consistency is reached.
5. Set the dough in the lightly oiled bowl, warp with a kitchen towel, and set aside for around an hour to rise.
6. To make a piloncillo, place it in the plastic bag and crush it with a hammer until it is finely ground.
7. Divide the crushed piloncillo into two parts. In a small bowl, combine half of the piloncillo with 1 teaspoon of flour. Before baking, this will be used to top the semitas.
8. After the dough has risen, add the pecans, orange zest, and the remaining half of the piloncillo. Knead the dough until all the ingredients are evenly mixed.
9. Warm the oven up to 350°F.
10. Now, cut the dough into 4 pieces, roll each piece tightly into a round, and put it on the sheet tray lined with parchment paper. Lightly press down on the rounds. Brush the rounds with your preferred plant milk, then sprinkle with the piloncillo and flour mixture. Using your hands, lightly press down on the piloncillo topping.
11. After that, allow the dough to rise for about 20 minutes on the sheet tray covered with a kitchen towel.
12. Bake at 350° for 20 minutes.

26. Molletes (Mexican Anise Seed Rolls)

Prep Time: 30-35 Minutes / Cook Time: 20-25 Minutes / Total Time: 2-3 Hours / Yield: 24 rolls

Ingredients

- 1 package of active dry yeast
- 1 1/2 cups sugar
- 2 eggs
- 2 tablespoons sugar
- 2 cups warm water (105°-115°F)
- 1 teaspoon of anise seed
- margarine
- 6 -7cups flour
- 1/2cup shortening
- 1 teaspoon salt

Instructions

1. First, in a large bowl, mix warm water with yeast and 2 tablespoons of sugar. Set this mixture aside.
2. Cream shortening and remaining sugar in a medium-sized mixing bowl.
3. Add the eggs, salt, and anise seed and mix them in.
4. Add the creamed mixture to the yeast and mix it well.
5. Add flour gradually to the mixture until a moderately firm dough forms.
6. Using a lightly floured board, knead the dough until it becomes elastic and smooth.
7. Cover the dough in the greased bowl and let it rise until it doubles in size.
8. Punch down the dough, knead it, and allow it to double in size again.
9. Knead the dough and roll it into round balls the size of an egg.
10. Warm the oven up to 375°F.
11. Put it in a pan that has been greased, cover it, and let it double in size again.
12. Brush with margarine and bake for twenty to twenty-five minutes.

27. No-Knead Green Chile Cheese Bread

Prep Time: 5 Minutes / Cook Time: 55 Minutes / Rising Time: 4 Hours / Total Time: 5 Hours / Yield: 12

Ingredients

- 1 cup of shredded cheese (recommend queso Oaxaca or Monterey Jack)
- 1/2 cup of warm water (105-115 degrees F.)
- 3 tablespoons of Land O Lakes Butter with Olive Oil & Sea Salt, melted
- 1/4 teaspoon granulated sugar
- 1 teaspoon sea salt
- 1/4-ounce active dry yeast packet
- 1 tablespoon of Land O Lakes Butter with Olive Oil & Sea Salt, room temperature
- 3 cups all-purpose flour
- 1/2 cup milk, lukewarm
- 1 cup of roasted green chiles, peeled and chopped (about 4 chiles)

Instructions

1. Mix yeast with sugar and warm water. Mix everything together well. Allow it to sit for 10 minutes so the yeast can start to work.
2. Mix the yeast mixture with warm milk and 1 tablespoon of Land O'Lakes Butter with Olive Oil and Sea Salt in a stand mixer with a dough hook. Mix in the cheese and green chiles until everything is well mixed.
3. Add the flour slowly, then the salt, and mix the ingredients together until they are well blended. The dough will be a little sticky.
4. Place the dough in a bowl that has been greased. Warp the bowl with the tea towel and let it rise for two to four hours or until it doubles in size.
5. Warm the oven up to 375 degrees F.
6. Remove the dough from the bowl and place it on a floured surface. Still, the dough should be a little loose.
7. Now, spray some cooking spray on the loaf pan.
8. Carefully put the dough into the loaf pan so that it's spread out evenly. Put the dough in a loaf pan and cover it with a tea towel. Let it sit for up to 30 minutes while the oven heats up.
9. Spread melted Land O'Lakes butter with olive oil and sea salt over the dough.
10. Bake the loaf for about 45–55 minutes, or until golden brown.
11. Take the loaf out of the pan and set it on a rack to cool. Then, cut it into pieces. Put a tea towel over it to keep it warm.

28. No-Knead Mexican Bread

Prep Time: 29 Minutes / Cook Time: 45 Minutes / Rising Time: 18 Hours / Total Time: 19 Hours 5 Minutes / Yield: 1 large loaf

Ingredients

- ¼ teaspoon instant yeast
- 3⅓ cups of all-purpose flour, plus more for dusting
- 2 teaspoons kosher salt
- 1½ cups water, slightly warm
- 1 cup roasted, peeled, seeded, and finely chopped green Chile, hot or mild (thawed and well drained if frozen)
- 2 teaspoons Mexican oregano
- Cornmeal, as needed

Instructions

1. Mix the yeast, salt, Mexican oregano, and flour in a large bowl. Combine green chile with water, then add flour and mix well. Mix with the wooden spoon until everything is well combined. The dough will be flaky and sticky. Use plastic wrap to protect the bowl. Set the dough to rise at room temperature for 18 hours.
2. Put some flour on a pastry or cutting board, then put the dough on it. After adding a bit more flour, fold it over on itself once or twice. You can use a spatula because the dough will be sticky. Put some loose plastic wrap around it and let it rest for 15 minutes.
3. Now, flour your hands and quickly shape the dough into a ball (or halve it to make 2 smaller loaves). Cover a large piece of waxed or parchment paper with cornmeal and put the dough on it, seam side down. Add more cornmeal to the dust. Allow it to rise for two hours, covered with plastic wrap.
4. Preheat the oven to 450° for about a half hour before the dough is ready. Place a 6- to 8-quart heavy pot (or use two smaller pots) with a lid (cast iron, Pyrex, enamel, or ceramic) in the oven while it heats.
5. When the dough is ready, take the pot out of the oven with care. Lift the dough with your hand under the paper and flip it seam-side up into the pot. Shake the pan once or twice to spread it out evenly.
6. Place the lid on top, and bake for 30 minutes. After that, take off the lid and cook for another 15 minutes, or until the loaf is toasty brown. Allow it to cool on a rack.

29. Ojos de Buey Pan (Sweet Bread)

Prep Time: 2 Hours / Cook Time: 20 Minutes / Total Time: 2 Hours 20 Minutes / Yield: 20 ojos

Ingredients
For the Dough:

- 3 cups bread flour, for rolling out
- 1 tsp salt
- ¾ cup granulated sugar, for coating the strips
- 4 ⅛ cups bread flour
- 1 ⅓ cups unsalted butter, at room temperature
- 3 tsp fast-action yeast
- 1 cup warm water
- 1 tsp vanilla extract

For the Cake Filling:

- ¾ cup unsalted butter, melted
- 2 large eggs, at room temperature
- 2 tbsp baking powder
- ¼ cup whole milk
- 2 tbsp orange zest
- 1 ⅓ cup granulated sugar
- 2 ¾ cups all-purpose flour
- ⅔ cup light-tasting olive oil

Instructions
Making the Dough:

1. Put the bread flour in a bowl, and along the sides of the bowl, put the salt and yeast. Make sure to keep each one separate as you stir them in.
2. Mix the warm water and vanilla extract together to make a dough. Add more water if it looks a little dry. Add more flour if the dough looks a little wet. For this recipe, remember that you want the dough to be dry, with some flour still in the bowl.
3. Put the dough on a surface that hasn't been floured and knead it for 5 to 10 minutes to bring it together. The dough needs to be very smooth and stretchy.
4. Cut the butter into cubes and split them into three equal parts.
5. Make a circle with the dough and sprinkle ⅓ of the butter over it. Knead the dough for a few minutes or until all the butter is mixed in. Do it again for the second part, and then for the third. At some point, the dough will get more buttery and sticky, so if you need to, use a bench scraper to fold it over on itself.
6. Incorporate some of the extra 3 cups of flour slowly, using the bench scraper if needed. You might not need all of the flour; you just want the dough to be soft and flexible without being too sticky.
7. Put the dough in a bowl that has been floured, and then sprinkle more flour on top of it. Place it somewhere warm and cover it with a clean tea towel. Let it rise for about 45 minutes, or until it doubles in size.

Shaping the Rings:

1. Place the dough on a floured surface and gently knead it. It will be easier to work with the dough than before, but it will still be soft and a little sticky.
2. Use a kitchen scale to make sure the pieces of dough are all the same size.
3. Sprinkle flour on the work surface and roll out one of the pieces into a long, thin rectangular that is 10 to 11 inches (25 to 30 cm) long. Fold the dough into three parts, as if it were a business letter, and then turn it 90 degrees. Roll into a rectangle and fold again. This will make the dough have layers.
4. Again, roll out the dough into a rectangle, then neaten the ends by trimming them. To get two strips, cut it in half along the length. Spread sugar on both sides of the strips, and then pinch the ends of the strips together firmly to make two rings of dough.
5. Place the rings on a cookie sheet that lined with parchment paper about 3 inches apart. Chill in the fridge until you're ready to bake. Do steps 3–5 again with the rest of the pieces.

Making the Filling:

1. Put everything for the cake except the oil and melted butter into a medium-sized bowl. Use a spatula to mix them together until you get a dry paste.
2. Use an electric hand mixer, blend the butter and oil into the mixture until it is very smooth. Add a few tbsp milk to thin out the batter if it's too thick. When the batter is the right consistency, it should fall from the beaters in a long ribbon.
3. Look into the batter to see if any sugar grains remain. If so, keep beating for another 30 seconds to break up the sugar. When the batter is done, it should easily slide off a spoon, but it should be thick and form a V when it does.
4. Put half of the batter into each chilled ring.
5. In a 400F oven, bake for 20 to 25 minutes. Stick a toothpick into the middle of the cake and it should come out clean. That means the ojos are done.
6. On a wire rack, let the ojos cool for at least 20 minutes. Then, serve them with a hot coffee.

30. Orejas (Ear Bread)

Prep Time: 55 Minutes / Cook Time: 25 Minutes / Total Time: 1 Hour 20 Minutes / Yield: 18

Ingredients

- 2 tbsp ground cinnamon
- 1 cup sugar
- 2 sheets puff pastry

Instructions

1. If the puff pastry was frozen, let it thaw on the counter. For about 30 minutes.
2. Take a mixing bowl, then mix the cinnamon and sugar together.
3. Spread the sugar and cinnamon mix out evenly on a surface.
4. Open the puff pastry over the cinnamon sugar mixture.
5. Add more sugar and cinnamon to the top of the dough.
6. Now, roll out gently with a rolling pin to press the sugar into the dough.
7. Fold over the right side of the rectangle by about 1 inch.
8. Fold approximately 1 inch of the left side.
9. As you fold, sprinkle with the cinnamon-sugar mixture.
10. Now, press the cinnamon and sugar into the dough.
11. Keep folding the dough until it's all in one long, flat piece.
12. Make 1-inch pieces.
13. Use the cinnamon-sugar mix to coat each piece.
14. Put them on a pan and put them in the fridge for 15 minutes.
15. Do the same thing with the second puff pastry sheet.
16. Preheat the oven to 375 degrees F.
17. Take it out of the fridge.
18. Bake for 20 minutes.
19. After flipping, bake for another 5 minutes.

31. Pambazo Mexicano (Chorizo Potato Sandwich)

Prep Time: 20 Minutes / Cook Time: 25 Minutes / Total Time: 45 Minutes / Yield: 6 Pambazos

Ingredients

- 1 ½ cup of shredded iceberg lettuce
- 8 black peppercorns
- 2 chorizos 3 oz. each
- ¼ cup crumbled cheese
- ½ tsp Mexican oregano
- 6 Teleras or Kaiser rolls sliced lengthwise
- 3 guajillo peppers seeds, and veins removed
- 2 tbsp Mexican cream
- 1 garlic clove
- 2 ½ cups potatoes, diced
- 2 tbsp vegetable oil
- Salt to taste

Instructions

1. Add diced potatoes and hot water in a saucepan, and cook them over medium-high heat. The potatoes will be done in 10 to 12 minutes.
2. While the potatoes are cooking, put the guajillo peppers in a bowl with hot water. This will soften them up.
3. Meanwhile, heat your skillet over medium-high heat and cook the chorizo. It'll be ready in eight minutes.
4. The potatoes should be done by now, so remove them from the heat and drain. Combine them with the chorizo in the pan and cook for three minutes. This is just enough time for the flavors to combine and the potatoes to soften slightly. Set aside.
5. In a blender, mix guajillo peppers, garlic clove, oregano, peppercorns, and 1 cup of soaking water. Mix all of the ingredients together until the sauce is smooth. After straining, put it in a bowl.
6. Put in ½ tablespoon of oil and heat up a griddle. Turn the sliced rolls upside down and brush the tops with the Guajillo salsa all over. Flip the rolls so that the tops are warm and crispy. It will take about a minute on each side for this step. Do this again with the rest of the rolls, adding more oil to the pan as needed.
7. Put some chorizo and potatoes on each toasted roll, then add the shredded lettuce, cream, and cheese on top. Serve with pickled jalapenos or hot salsa. Enjoy!

32. Pan Casero de Manzana (Apple Bread)

Prep Time: 20 Minutes / Cook Time: 60 Minutes / Resting Time: 15 Minutes / Total Time: 1 Hour 35 Minutes / Yield: 1 loaf

Ingredients

- 3 cups green apple chopped into small cubes
- 1 tsp baking soda
- 2 tbsp ground cinnamon
- 3 cups all-purpose flour, sifted
- 1 cup golden raisins
- 1 1/4 cup oil (vegetable or canola oil work well)
- 1/2 tsp salt
- 2 tbsp pure vanilla extract
- 4 large eggs
- 1 tsp baking powder
- 3 cups sugar
- 1/4 tsp ground clove
- 1 cup chopped pecans or walnuts

Instructions

1. Heat the oven up to 325 degrees.
2. Prepare a 13-by-9-inch glass baking dish by greasing it and set aside. I like to grease my dish with a combination of butter and flour.
3. Put the flour, sugar, salt, cinnamon, baking soda, clove, and baking powder in a large bowl and mix them together.
4. Using a hand mixer, add the oil, vanilla extract, and egg's part by part. About 60 seconds later, when the dry and wet ingredients are well mixed, add the chopped apples, raisins, and nuts. Continue mixing for an extra 45 seconds or until all the ingredients are well mixed.
5. Now, pour the mixture into greased baking dish.
6. Bake at 325°F for one hour, or until a toothpick inserted into the center of the bread comes out clean. The bread should have a slightly crispy top at this point, but the inside remains moist.
7. Let it cool down, and then carefully flip it over onto a different rectangular dish. Before flipping it, loosen the edges with a butter knife.
8. Garnish with sliced apples, powdered sugar, and honey.

33. Pan de Calabaza (Pumpkin Bread)

Prep Time: 10 Minutes / Cook Time: 60 Minutes / Total Time: 1 Hour 10 Minutes / Yield: 12 slices

Ingredients

- 1 ½ cups pumpkin puree
- 1 ¾ cups all-purpose flour
- 2 eggs at room temperature
- 1 tsp pumpkin spice mix
- 1 tsp baking soda
- ½ cup vegetable oil
- ½ cup light or dark brown sugar
- ¼ cup buttermilk (or milk)
- ¾ tsp salt
- 2 tsp ground cinnamon
- ¾ cups sugar
- ½-⅔ cups semi-sweet chocolate chips, optional
- 3 tbsp chopped pecans, optional

Instructions

1. Preheat the oven to 350°.
2. Combine the flour, baking soda, cinnamon, and pumpkin spice mix in a medium-sized bowl. Mix everything together.
3. Put the eggs, sugar, and brown sugar in a different bowl. Blend everything together with a whisk.
4. Put in the pumpkin puree, buttermilk, and oil. Combine the ingredients slowly by whisking them together.
5. Now add the mixture to the dry flour mixture. Mix slowly with a whisk.
6. Do not whisk too hard or too rough! There will be some lumps, that's okay. Don't mix it excessively!
7. Put in chocolate chips and chopped pecans. Add to the mixture.
8. Use a little butter, spray, or oil to grease a 9x5-inch loaf pan.
9. Put the mix in the pan.
10. Put it in the oven at 350° for 60 to 65 minutes. Keep in mind that every oven is different, so check your bread after 55 minutes by putting a toothpick or thin butter knife in the middle of the loaf.
11. When you stick a toothpick or butter knife into the middle of bread, and if it comes out clean, the bread is done.
12. Let the bread rest in the loaf pan for at least 10 minutes before taking it out. You can finish cooling it on a wire rack or leave it in the pan.
13. Cut it into 1-inch slices when you're ready to serve. Enjoy!

34. Pan de Canela (Cinnamon Bread)

Prep Time: 30 Minutes / Cook Time: 20 Minutes / Proof Time: 30 Minutes / Total Time: 1 Hour 20 Minutes / Yield: 8 servings

Ingredients:

- 2 tsps vanilla extract
- 1/2 cup lukewarm water
- 3/4 cup (167 grams) of unsalted butter, at room temperature

Dry Ingredients:

- 1/2 lb (225 grams) all-purpose flour
- 1/3 cup (45 grams) granulated sugar
- 1 1/2 tablespoons (15 grams) active dry yeast
- 1 1/4 tablespoons (10 grams) baking powder
- 2 3/4 tbsps (15 grams) fresh ground canel, cinnamon
- 1/2 cup more granulated sugar for dredging bread once baked

Instructions:

1. In the stand mixer bowl, mix all the dry ingredients together. Whisk until everything is well combined.
2. Melt the butter and cut it in until you get small crumbles. Add the vanilla and stir. Mix the 1/2 cup of water in slowly. Knead the dough for 5-7 minutes on medium/low speed. The dough shouldn't stick to your hands, but it should feel sticky.
3. Now, place dough on a lightly floured flat surface. Use just enough flour to make the dough workable. Then, roll each piece into a ball and divide it into 8 equal parts.
4. Line a baking sheet with parchment paper. Set aside.
5. Take each ball of dough and roll it out gently to form an oval shape that is approximately 4 1/2 inches long. To make a design, cut the dough all the way up with a serrated knife. To score, hold the knife at an angle. Just be careful not to cut all the way through the dough.
6. Carefully flip the scored dough over. You could now add the traditional filling, which is the candy paste used for concha topping. At this point, I chose not to add any filling.
7. With both hands, start rolling in from the edge closest to you. Put light pressure on the ends as you roll to make them taper. Place on a lined baking sheet. Now, set the oven to 350 degrees and bake for about 20 to 23 minutes. Not all ovens are the same. Remove from the oven when done and immediately coat the warm bread in granulated sugar. Allow for a 10-minute resting period. Enjoy.

35. Pan de Plátano (Banana Bread)

Prep Time: 15 Minutes / Cook Time: 50 Minutes / Total Time: 65 Minutes / Yield: 8-10 slices

Ingredients

- 2 large eggs, beaten
- 140g self-rising flour
- 1 tsp baking powder
- 50g icing sugar
- 140g caster sugar
- 140g of butter, softened, plus extra for the tin
- 2 very ripe bananas, mashed
- handful dried banana chips, for decoration

Instructions

1. Preheat the oven to 180C/160C fan/gas 4.
2. Butter a 2-pound loaf pan and put baking parchment around the sides and base.
3. Cream together softened butter and caster sugar until light and fluffy, then gradually add in eggs and a little of the 140g flour.
4. Add the rest of the flour, 1 tsp of baking powder, and 2 mashed bananas.
5. Then, pour mixture into the prepared tin and bake for about 50 minutes or until thoroughly cooked. From about 30 to 40 minutes in the oven, test the loaf every 5 minutes with a skewer (it should go in and out cleanly). The time may change depending on the shape of your loaf tin because it will bake at different rates.
6. Let it cool in the pan for 10 minutes, then move it to a wire rack.
7. To make a runny icing, mix 50 grams of icing sugar with two to three tablespoons of water.
8. If you want to decorate the cake, add a handful of banana chips and drizzle the icing over the top.

36. Pan de Muertos (Mexican Bread of the Dead)

Prep Time: 25 Minutes / Cook Time: 45 Minutes / Additional Time: 2 Hours / Total Time: 3 Hours 10 Minutes / Yield: 12 slices (1 loaf)

Ingredients:

Bread:

- 2 large eggs, beaten
- 2 tsp anise seed
- ¼ cup white sugar
- 3 cups all-purpose flour
- ¼ cup butter or margarine
- ¼ cup of warm water (110 degrees F/45 degrees C)
- 1 tbsp orange zest
- ¼ cup milk
- ½ tsp salt
- 1 ¼ tsp active dry yeast

Glaze:

- 2 tbsp white sugar
- 2 tsp orange zest
- ¼ cup orange juice
- ¼ cup white sugar

Instructions:

To make the bread:

1. Take a medium saucepan, then heat the milk and the butter over low heat until butter melts. Take it off the heat and add warm water. The mixture should be around 110 degrees Fahrenheit (43 degrees Celsius).
2. Take a large bowl, then mix 1 cup of flour, yeast, anise seed, sugar, and salt. Add eggs and orange zest and beat them in until everything is well mixed. Then, add 1/2 cup flour and mix it in. Continue add flour until the dough is soft.
3. Now, spread the dough out on a lightly floured surface, then knead it until it is smooth and elastic. Then, spread some oil in a bowl and put the dough in it. Let it rise in a warm place for one to two hours, then cover it with plastic wrap.
4. Punch down the dough, then shape it into a large round loaf with a round knob on top. Place dough on a baking sheet and cover it loosely with plastic wrap. Then put the dough somewhere warm and let it rise until it almost doubles in size. This should take about an hour.
5. Preheat the oven on to 350 degrees F (175 degrees C).
6. Preheat oven and bake for about 35 to 45 minutes, or until golden brown. Allow to cool slightly before glazing.

To make the glaze:

9. In a small saucepan, mix white sugar, orange juice, and orange zest. Boil for two minutes over medium-low heat. Spread the glaze on top of the warm bread. Just add two tablespoons of sugar on top.

37. Pan de Yema (Egg Yolk Bread)

Prep Time: 30 Minutes / Cook Time: 3 Hours 20 Minutes / Total Time: 3 Hours 50 Minutes / Yield: 16 Buns

Ingredients

- 9 egg yolks
- 6 cups of all-purpose flour, divided, plus more for dough shaping
- 3 envelopes of active dry yeast granules
- Pinch of kosher or coarse sea salt
- 2/3 cup sugar, plus 1 teaspoon
- 1 cup of unsalted butter, plus more for greasing
- 2 large eggs plus 1 for egg wash
- 1 1/4 cup lukewarm water

Instructions

1. Combine the yeast granules, 1 teaspoon of sugar, and lukewarm water in a small bowl. The water should not be too hot or too cold for the yeast to react. After mixing, put it somewhere warm in your kitchen so that it won't get cold drafts. After a few minutes, mix it again to make it dissolve. Continue to leave it alone for a few more minutes, until the mixture reacts and the top looks foamy. Add 1 cup flour and mix them well. Wrap it in a clean kitchen towel and set them aside for an hour to rise.
2. With the paddle attachment on a mixer, beat the butter and 2/3 cup sugar on medium speed until butter soft and creamy. Lower the speed and add egg yolks, 2 eggs, rest of the flour, and a pinch of salt to the yeast mixture.
3. After a few minutes, replace the paddle attachment with the hook attachment. In a bowl, mix the dough on low to medium speed with a stand mixer for about 10 to 12 minutes, or until it is very soft, smooth, and shiny, and you can shape it into a ball.
4. Butter a large bowl. Form a ball with the dough and put it in the bowl. Place it in a warm spot in your kitchen that doesn't get drafty and cover it with a dish towel. Wait an hour or so until it doubles in size.
5. Preheat oven to 350 degrees Fahrenheit and grease three baking sheets.
6. Uncover and punch down the dough. Cut it in half, then each of the two halves in turn until you have sixteen pieces of dough. Create a ball out of each one and place it on the baking sheets that have been greased. Place in a warm spot in your kitchen for 45 minutes to an hour to give it one last rise.
7. Using a small bowl, beat the last egg with a tablespoon of water. Make three cuts in the top of each bun and use egg wash to cover them.

8. Bake for 20 minutes, or until they are fully cooked and the top is browned.

38. Pan Margaritas (Bread Rolls)

Prep Time: 30 Minutes / Cook Time: 23 Minutes / Proof Time: 1 Hour 10 Minutes / Total Time: 2 Hour 3 Minutes / Yield: 8 rolls

Ingredients

- 1 1/2 cups room temperature water
- 10 grams salt, (1 3/4 tsps)
- 12 grams active dry yeast, (4 tsps)
- 12 grams sugar, (2 1/2 tsps)
- 12 grams of shortening, plus 20 grams more for later (2 1/2 tablespoons total)
- 3 cups of bread flour or all-purpose flour, plus 1/4 cup for dusting about 388 grams of flour total

Instructions

1. Put the yeast, sugar, salt, and 360 grams of flour in a large, shallow bowl. To make fine crumbles, cut 1 tablespoon shortening into the dry ingredients with a fork or your hand.
2. Heat the oven up to 200 degrees F. After it reaches the right temperature, turn off the oven.
3. Mix the water in slowly. It's going to be sticky. Wait a little while longer and keep kneading the dough for another 10 minutes. Don't put in any more flour.
4. Then, you need turn the dough out onto a lightly floured surface and roll them into a ball. Place in a greased bowl. Let it sit in the semi-warm oven for 30 minutes, covered, until it has almost doubled in size.
5. Move the dough to your work surface when it's ready. Oil your hands to make it easier to work with the dough. Work the dough for one minute. Now, cut dough into 8 equal pieces using a pastry cutter or a large knife. Put 8 dough balls on a baking sheet that has been greased.
6. Take a little of the remaining shortening at a time and gently flatten and turn each margarita around so it looks like a thick pancake. Don't be shy to use shortening. Once all of them are done, cover them again and put them back in the oven that is semi-warm for another 30 to 40 minutes to proof.
7. Take the margaritas out of the oven once they have risen. Warm the oven up to 380 degrees F. When the oven reaches temperature, uncover the margaritas and place them in the center section. For 21 to 23 minutes, or until light golden brown. Take it out of the oven and let it cool for 5 minutes before cutting it open. In a plastic bag, you can keep cooled margaritas for a few days.

39. Pan Dulce de Elotes (Corn Shape Sweetbread)

Prep Time: 45 Minutes / Cook Time: 20 Minutes / Resting Time: 1 Hour / Total Time: 2 Hours 5 Minutes / Yield: 15 Elotes

Ingredients
For Dough:

- 2 cups flour
- 1/4 cup warm water
- 1/3 cup sugar
- 1 tsp cinnamon
- 1 large egg slightly beaten
- 1 tsp active dry yeast
- 1/2 cup shortening
- 1/2 tsp salt
- 1/2 tsp ground anise, optional

For Filling:

- 1/2 tsp cinnamon
- 1 egg yolk
- 2/3 cup flour
- 1/2 cup powdered sugar
- 1/2 cup softened butter
- 2 drops of yellow food coloring optional
- Zest of 1 orange optional
- More sugar for dusting

Instructions

1. Put the two cups of flour on a flat surface or a big cutting board. Add 1 tsp yeast, 1/2 tsp salt, and 1/3 cup sugar to the flour. Use your hands to mix the ingredients together. Add the egg and mix it in with your fingers. Add the water gently; the dough will be lumpy. Put the shortening, cinnamon, and anise. For about 5 to 7 minutes, knead the dough until it is smooth. For 30 minutes, cover and leave alone.
2. Preheat oven to 375 degrees F. Then, add parchment paper on a baking sheet and set it aside.
3. Combine all the filling ingredients in a different bowl. Use your hands to mix until dough forms. Shape 15 small balls into a cigar shape by rolling them between your palms. The cigar should be about 2 inches long. Place on a plate, cover, and set aside.
4. With the dough you saved, make 15 balls that are all the same size. With wax paper on the inside of a tortilla press, press the dough ball out to about 3 inches. Cut straight lines across the flattened dough with a knife or metal spatula. Score it again so it goes across the other lines when you turn it over.
5. Carefully turn it over and add the filling down the middle. Fold the sides in and press to seal. Make the end look almost like an ear of corn by pinching it together.
6. Line a baking sheet and put the seam side down on it. Sprinkle with sugar. For 30 minutes, cover and leave alone. Place pan in a hot oven and bake for about 20 minutes, turning it over halfway through. Bake until it turns golden. Place in an airtight container after letting it cool completely.

40. Pan Dulces (Mexican Sweet Buns)

Prep Time: 30 Minutes / Cook Time: 20 Minutes / Additional Time: 1 Hour 40 Minutes / Total Time: 2 Hours 30 Minutes / Yield: 16 buns

Ingredients

- 1 (.25 ounce) package active dry yeast
- ⅓ cup white sugar
- ½ cup white sugar
- cooking spray
- 2 egg yolks
- 4 tbsp butter, softened
- 2 large eggs
- 5 cups all-purpose flour
- ⅔ cup all-purpose flour
- 1 cup milk
- 1 tsp salt
- 6 tbsp butter

Instructions

1. Put milk in a small saucepan and heat it until it bubbles. Then take it off the heat. Mix in the butter and pour into a large bowl to cool.
2. Mix the yeast into the milk. Include 1/3 cup of sugar and salt. Include 2 cups of flour and the eggs. Add rest of the flour, 1/2 cup at a time, beating well after each addition. Once the dough has come together, put it on a lightly floured surface and knead it for about 8 minutes, until it is smooth and soft. Put a little oil in a big bowl, then put the dough in it and turn it around to coat it with oil. Put a damp cloth over it and let it rise in a warm place for about an hour, or until it has doubled in size.
3. Now, cut the dough into 16 equal pieces, and then roll each one out into a round shape. Using a rolling pin, make oval buns out of the rounds. After lightly greasing two baking sheets, place them on. Put a damp cloth over the rolls and let them rise for about 40 minutes, or until they have doubled in size.
4. Set the oven temperature at 350 degrees F (175 degrees C).
5. Get the topping ready while the bread rises: Make a crumb mixture by mixing 1/2 cup of sugar, 2/3 cup of flour, and butter in a small bowl. It's important to mix the egg yolks in well. Cover the whole surface of the rolls with the crumbled topping.
6. After the oven is hot, bake for 15 to 20 minutes, or until the sugar topping starts to turn a light brown.

41. Polvorones (Mexican Wedding Cookies)

Prep Time: 20 Minutes / Cook Time: 15 Minutes / Total Time: 35 Minutes / Yield: 3 dozen Cookies

Ingredients

- 3 ounces chopped pecans
- 1 cup butter, room temperature
- 1 tbsp of vanilla bean paste or pure vanilla extract
- 1 cup of powdered sugar, sifted plus 1/4 cup for topping
- 2 cups all-purpose flour, sifted
- 1/2 tsp kosher salt

Instructions

1. Preheat the oven to 325 degrees F.
2. Put 3 ounces of pecans in a prep dish and chop them up very small. Set them aside.
3. Now, add 1 cup of butter, 1 cup of powdered sugar, and salt to the stand mixer. Then, use the paddle attachment to mix them together. To keep powdered sugar from flying out of the bowl, start the machine on a low speed and slowly raise it to medium speed.
4. Now, add vanilla bean paste or vanilla extract and keep mixing on medium speed until it's all mixed in.
5. Lowered the mixer's speed and added the sifted flour slowly, about 1/4 cup at a time, until it was all mixed in.
6. Mix in the chopped pecans until they are fully mixed in.
7. Form the dough into rounded tablespoons and roll them into balls.
8. Now, put them on a baking sheet lined with parchment paper then you need to bake them at 325 degrees Fahrenheit for about 13 to 15 minutes. Unless they are over-baked, the cookies' tops don't get brown, so the dough should still look very light when they are done.
9. Take the cookies out of the oven and let them cool for 15 minutes. Then, sprinkle the rest of the powdered sugar on top of them.

42. Pink Pan Dulce (Pink Sweet Bread)

Prep Time: 30 Minutes / Cook Time: 18-20 Minutes / Total Time: 2 Hours 20 Minutes / Yield: 16 buns

Ingredients
For the Dough:

- 4 Eggs
- 1/2 cup Granulated Sugar
- 2 cups Bread Flour
- 1 tsp Salt
- 2 tbsp Granulated Sugar
- 1/2 cup Butter, melted
- 1 tbsp Active Dry Yeast
- 3 1/4 cups All-Purpose Flour
- 1 cup Evaporated Milk

For the Topping:

- 1 tsp Almond Extract
- 3 drops Americolor Dusty Rose Food Coloring
- 1/2 tsp Baking Soda
- 1 1/2 cups Powdered Confectioners Sugar
- 1 tbsp Half and Half
- 1/2 tbsp Vanilla Extract
- 1 pinch Salt
- 3 cups All-Purpose Flour
- 1 1/2 cups Butter, room temperature

Instructions
1. Warm the evaporated milk until it reaches 100 to 110 degrees F (38 to 43 degrees C). Then, you need add the sugar and active dry yeast. Leave it alone for about 10 minutes, or until the top starts to foam.
2. Now, mix the eggs and granulated sugar in a large stand mixer. Then, pour in the yeast mixture and whisk to combine. Add the butter gradually until it's well mixed in.
3. It's time to add the bread dough hook to the mixer. Next, add the salt, all-purpose flour, and bread flour. Turn speed to medium and knead the dough for a few minutes, or until it comes together.
4. The dough should stick to the bottom but come off the sides of the bowl. Add All-purpose flour one tbsp at a time if the dough isn't pulling away from the sides. Then, knead dough on medium speed for another ten minutes.
5. Take the dough out of the bowl and put it in a clean, greased bowl. Turn the dough over once to coat it. Place a plastic wrap over it and give it an hour to rise.
6. Start by cutting the dough in half. Then, keep cutting each piece in half until you have 16 pieces of dough.
7. Roll out each piece of dough and wrap the sides around to the middle of the bottom. Keep doing this until you have a clean ball. Now, place on a lined cookie sheet then cover with a clean towel while you prepare the topping.
8. Warm the oven up to 190 degrees C (375 degrees F).
9. Mix the powdered sugar, food coloring, almond extract, and vanilla extract with the butter until the mixture is smooth, which should take about one to two minutes.
10. Mix the All-Purpose Flour, Baking Soda, and 1 pinch of salt in slowly until the mixture is crumbly.
11. Add the half-and-half and mix it in well until it's all the same.
12. Turn out onto a clean work surface. Top it with wax or parchment paper and roll it out until it's about 1/4 inch thick. Use a 4-inch biscuit cutter to make the shapes.
13. After cutting shell shapes out of the rounds, put them on top of the dough balls and press down on the sides.
14. Put it in the oven and bake for about 18 to 20 minutes, or until a thermometer inside reads 190 degrees F (88 degrees C).
15. Let it cool down a bit, and then serve it hot.

43. Pumpkin Conchas (Pumpkin Sweet Bread)

Prep Time: 30 Minutes / Cook Time: 20 Minutes / Rise Time: 3 Hours / Total Time: 3 Hours 50 Minutes / Yield: 6

Ingredients

Dough:

- 1 large egg yolk
- 2 ¼ cups all-purpose flour
- ¼ cup warm milk
- 2 tbsp white sugar
- 1 tsp kosher salt
- ½ cup pumpkin puree
- 1 (.25 ounce) package active dry yeast
- ⅛ tsp vanilla extract
- 2 tbsp butter, melted

Topping:

- ¼ cup butter, at room temperature
- ¼ tsp ground cinnamon
- 1 pinch kosher salt
- ⅛ tsp ground allspice
- ½ cup all-purpose flour
- ½ cup powdered sugar
- ⅛ tsp vanilla extract
- 1 pinch ground nutmeg
- Orange food coloring (Optional)

Instructions

1. Take a bowl of a stand mixer fitted with a dough hook, mix flour, pumpkin puree, warm milk, egg yolk, melted butter, sugar, active dry yeast, salt, and vanilla extract. Knead the dough by hand for about 5 minutes or until it forms a smooth, slightly stretchy ball.
2. Cover the dough in a bowl that has been lightly greased and set it in a warm place for about two hours, or until it has doubled in size.
3. As the dough rises, make the topping by combining powdered sugar, flour, butter, cinnamon, allspice, nutmeg, salt, and vanilla extract in a bowl. By hand or with a spatula, mix until a dough that you can shape comes together. Add orange food coloring (optional).
4. Make 6 equal portions of topping dough and roll each one into a ball. Now, place the balls on a baking sheet lined with parchment paper. Overlay a piece of plastic over each ball and flatten them into a circle with the bottom of a glass or measuring cup or something else heavy and flat. Using the tip of a knife, cut a pumpkin design into the topping. Putting the butter in the fridge will make it firm up.
5. Once the dough has risen, put it on a work surface and press it down to get rid of the air. Now, divide dough into 6 equal pieces, then roll each piece into a smooth ball. add the balls on a baking sheet lined with Silpat and lightly press them down to make them flat. On top of the dough balls, put the topping. Let it rise for about 45 minutes, or until it doubles in size.
6. Warm up the oven to 190 degrees C (375 degrees F).
7. It will take about 20 minutes of baking in the middle of a hot oven until it's golden and puffed up. Give it about 20 minutes to cool down to room temperature.

44. Roles de Canela (Cinnamon Rolls)

Prep Time: 25 Minutes / Cook Time: 15 Minutes / Raising Time: 4 Hours / Total Time: 4 Hours 40 Minutes / Yield: 9 rolls

Ingredients:

For the bread:

- 40 grams unsalted butter, room temperature
- 100 grams whole milk
- 200 grams bread flour
- 1 1/2 teaspoons pure vanilla extract
- 1 large egg, room temperature
- 3 grams kosher salt
- 36 grams granulated sugar
- 5 grams fast-rise instant yeast

For the filling:

- 113 grams (8 tablespoons) unsalted butter, room temperature
- 1 teaspoon pure vanilla extract
- 2 1/2 tablespoons ground cinnamon
- 1 pinch kosher salt
- 1/3 cup dark brown sugar, packed
- 1/2 cup raw pecans, chopped

For the glaze:

- 1 cup of powdered sugar
- 1 1/2 tbsp of whole milk

For greasing the container where you'll proof the dough:

- Cooking spray

For flouring your work surface:

- All-purpose flour, as needed

Instructions:

1. In the bowl of a stand mixer, mix sugar, fast-rise instant yeast, and bread flour. With the dough hook attachment attached, set the mixer to speed 2 (slowest) and mix the dry ingredients.
2. Put in warm milk, one large egg, and butter. Turn the speed up to 4 (medium) and let it run for 5 minutes.
3. Add kosher salt and pure vanilla extract to the bowl. Mix on speed 4 for another 10 minutes, or until dough pulls away from the sides of the bowl and mostly gathers around the hook. You might have to stop the mixer sometimes to use a spatula to clean the sides. This way, you won't waste any dough.
4. Spray cooking spray on the inside of a large glass bowl or use 6-quart food container with a lid so the dough doesn't stick to the sides. This will be where the dough will rise.
5. It's time to proof and cover the dough. Move it from the bowl of the stand mixer to a bowl or other container. Do not touch the dough for about two hours, or until it has doubled in size.
6. Spread the dough out on a floured surface after it has doubled in size. Use just enough all-purpose flour so the dough doesn't stick to the surface. Roll it out slowly to 9x13 inches with a floured rolling pin. It's okay if your dough isn't a perfect rectangle.
7. Get the paddle attachment for your stand mixer and use it to make the filling. To start, cream the butter and sugar together. Then, add the kosher salt, ground cinnamon, and pure vanilla extract. On speed 4, mix until everything is well mixed.
8. Spread the filling mixture on the rolled-out dough, leaving 1/2 inch around the edges. Then, use a spoon or you can use offset spatula to spread pecans out evenly over the filling. Then, gently roll the dough from the long side inward. Tuck the seam of the dough under the roll.
9. Cut the dough into 9 equal pieces with a bench scraper or you can use a very sharp knife. Put them in a 9x9 pan lined with parchment paper then cover with a kitchen towel for the second rise. Let them rise until they double in size. It should take between 1.5 and 2 hours in total.
10. Take it out of the oven then let it cool for about 10 minutes before adding the icing. Let the icing set for 10 minutes, then serve immediately.

45. Rosca de Reyes (Three Kings Bread)

Prep Time: 30 Minutes / Cook Time: 25-30 Minutes / Total Time: 3-4 Hours / Yield: 12

Ingredients:

- 4 1/2 cups flour, divided
- 1/2 tsp salt
- 5 eggs, at room temperature, divided
- 1/4 cup of warm water, (105°F to 115°F)
- 1 1/4 tsp Ground Cinnamon, divided
- 1 envelope active dry yeast
- 1/2 cup confectioners' sugar
- 1/3 cup plus 1 tbsp of granulated sugar, divided
- 4 tsp Pure Orange Extract
- 1/3 cup of warm milk, (105°F to 115°F)
- 1 cup (2 sticks) of butter, softened, divided
- 1 egg yolk
- Candied dried fruit, such as figs, lemons, cherries, oranges, mango or pineapple
- Sliced almonds

Instructions:

1. Add yeast to a small bowl of warm water. Add one tbsp of the granulated sugar and mix it in. Wait 5 to 10 minutes, or until it foams up. In a medium size bowl, add 3/4 cup (1 1/2 sticks) butter and stir it in until it melts. Set aside.
2. Meanwhile, use a large mixer bowl with a dough hook attachment to mix 2 cups of flour, the last 1/3 cup of granulated sugar, 4 eggs, 1 teaspoon of cinnamon, and salt for one minute on low speed, or until everything is well mixed. Then add the orange extract, the milk and butter mixture, and the yeast mixture. Beat for two minutes. Now, slowly add the last two cups of flour, beating for two minutes. (The dough should be kind of soft and sticky.) Put the dough on a surface that has been lightly floured. Knead for five minutes, or until the dough is smooth and stretchy. (Dough shouldn't be dry; it should be soft and sticky.)
3. Butter or oil a bowl and put the dough in it. Roll out the dough in the bowl, making sure the greased side is facing up. Use buttered or oiled plastic wrap to cover the bowl. Position the bowl in a warm, draft-free area, like the microwave or an oven that has been turned off. If you want the dough to almost double in size, let it sit for one to two hours.
4. At the same time, use an electric mixer on medium speed to blend the last 1/4 cup butter and confectioners' sugar in a medium bowl. To make a smooth paste, add the last 1/2 cup of flour, the last 1/4 teaspoon of cinnamon, and the egg yolk. Cut into 6 equal pieces. Place plastic wrap around it. Set aside.
5. When the dough is almost doubled, press it down to get rid of the air. Take it out of the bowl and put it on a floured surface. Knead it a few times, and then roll it into a ball. Get the dough and roll it into a log that is 40 inches long and 2 inches wide. Now, place them on a large baking sheet lined with parchment paper. Shape the dough into a big oval ring by bringing the ends together. Using wet hands, press the ends together to seal them. Use a clean kitchen towel to cover. Place the baking sheet somewhere warm and draft-free. Wait another hour or two, or until the dough has almost doubled in size.
6. Set the oven to 350°F. Blend the remaining egg thoroughly by beating it. Apply a beaten egg to the dough ring. Roll the confectioners' sugar mixture into 3-inch-long by 1 1/2-inch-wide strips. Decoratively arrange the strips on the dough ring. You can add candied fruit pieces and sliced almonds as a garnish if you like.
7. Put it in the oven for 25 to 35 minutes, or until it turns golden brown and when you tap it, it sounds hollow. Cool all the way on the wire rack.

46. Telera Bread (Bread Roll)

Prep Time: 8 Minutes / Cook Time: 28 Minutes / Resting Time: 1 Hour 30 Minutes / Total Time: 2 Hours 6 Minutes / Yield: 8 Telera

Ingredients

- 4 (20 g) tsp sugar
- 1 1/2 tsp (10 g) salt
- 2 tsp (6-7 g) dry active yeast
- 1 1/3 cups (300 ml) warm water
- 1 1/2 tbsp (approx 25 g) softened unsalted butter
- 3 1/2 cups (500 g) all-purpose flour
- Little bit of oil to grease bowl

Instructions

1. Combine flour and salt on a clean surface, then create a well in the middle of it.
2. Add the yeast and a little sugar to the middle. Take a fork and mix in a little water. Then, let it sit for one minute. You'll see bubbles form in the yeast.
3. Mix the flour with a fork and keep adding water until it turns into a very wet batter in the middle. Leave some flour around the well's edge to keep the water in.
4. Put in the rest of the sugar and the chunks of butter. Start mixing the flour and butter together with your fingers. Then mix it all together until you have a rough ball that doesn't stick to your hands.
5. After that, knead for another four to five minutes or until the dough becomes soft. Put it in a bowl that has been greased, and then flip the ball over once to grease the top of it as well.
6. Put plastic wrap or a clean kitchen towel over it and let it sit for about 45 minutes to an hour, or until it doubles in size.
7. Take the dough out of the bowl and punch it to let the air out. Knead it for a few seconds and then cut it into 8 equal pieces, each about 100 g (3.5 oz). Using a towel, cover the balls and let them rest for 10 to 15 minutes.
8. Take one ball, gently pull at the sides, and then flatten it into an oval shape on a floured surface. Add a little more flour on top, and use your fingertips to shape it into an oval shape.
9. Put the plastic straw (or a thin rolling pin, a clean, round spoon handle, or even a clean, thicker writing pen) on top of the oval shape about one-third of the way from one edge. Firmly press down until it touches surface but doesn't cut the dough, then do the same thing with the other edge.
10. This will make the telera's traditional shape.
11. Repeat with the other 8, then put them on a parchment-lined baking sheet. Place a kitchen towel over them and let them rest for about 45 minutes, or until they have doubled in size.
12. Preheat oven to 200 C (400 F).
13. Using a pastry brush, add a little water to the top. Bake for 15 minutes, or until golden.

47. Telera Rolls

Prep Time: 35 Minutes / Cook Time: 20 Minutes / Total Time: 2 Hours 30 Minutes / Yield: 10 rolls

Ingredients
Dough:

- 2 tsp instant yeast
- 1 1/2 cups (340g) water
- 4 to 4 1/2 cups (480g to 540g) of All-Purpose Flour
- 1 tbsp honey
- 1 1/2 tsp (9g) table salt
- 1 tbsp lard, shortening, or butter, melted and cooled

Glaze:

- 1 egg, beaten with 1 tbsp water

Instructions

1. Mix the yeast, water, honey, melted fat, salt, and 4 cups flour in a large mixing bowl or your bread machine pan that is set to the dough cycle. Mix until you get a soft dough.
2. Check the dough's texture. If it sticks to your finger when you lightly touch it, add 1/4 cup of extra flour and mix for one more minute. It should be soft but not sticky when you check the dough again and add the last 1/4 cup of flour only if you need to.
3. In a stand mixer, knead it on medium speed for 6 to 8 minutes, or by hand for 10 minutes, until it's smooth and springy.
4. Let the dough rise for an hour, or until it doubles in size, or let the bread machine finish its cycle.
5. Once the dough has risen, let it go down a bit and cut it into 10 pieces. Roll each of piece into a ball then cover it.
6. Allow the rolls to rest for about 5 minutes before shaping them into a football shape, tapering toward the edges; the rolls should be around 5 1/2" long and 2" around at the center.
7. Put all of the rolls on a greased baking sheet or lined with parchment paper. Cover with greased plastic wrap. Meanwhile, preheat the oven to 400°F and let the rolls rise.
8. Once the rolls are almost twice as big, use egg wash to cover the tops and sides. Use a greased knife, slash the rolls twice parallel to each other. Firmly press down on each slice.
9. It's done when it's golden brown and a digital thermometer reads 190°F in the middle, after 20 to 22 minutes of baking. Take out of the oven and let cool completely before cutting.

48. Tortillas

Prep Time: 30 Minutes / Cook Time: 25 Minutes / Additional Time: 1 Hour / Total Time: 1 Hour 55 Minutes / Yield: 12 tortillas

Ingredients

- 3 cups all-purpose flour
- ¾ cup hot water
- 2 tsp baking powder
- 2 tsp salt
- ¾ cup shortening or lard

Instructions

1. Take a large mixing bowl, then mix the flour, baking powder, and salt together. Add shortening and mix it in by hand or with a pastry cutter until it turns into a crumbly mess. If the mixture doesn't look like crumbles, add one or two more tablespoons of shortening. Add 3/4 cup hot water, or just enough to make it moist.
2. You can knead the dough by hand or with a big fork. To get rid of any extra dough, rub it against the sides of the bowl. Just add a few more tbsp of flour until the dough turns into a soft round shape if it still sticks to the bowl's sides. Put a clean dish towel over the dough and let it rest for about an hour. This will help it work better.
3. Make 12 balls of dough that are all the same size. Spread some flour on a surface and roll out each ball until it is about 1/8-inch thick.
4. Set the cast iron skillet on medium heat.
5. Cook a tortilla in the preheated pan around 30 seconds to 1 minute, or you need to cook until browned and slightly puffy. For the second side to brown, flip the tortilla over and cook for another 30 seconds to 1 minute. Then, move it to a plate. Do it again with every dough ball. Cover cooked tortillas with a towel to keep them warm and wet until you're ready to serve them.

49. Vanilla and Chocolate Conchas (Sweet Bread)

Prep Time: 30 Minutes / Cook Time: 15 Minutes / Additional Time: 2 Hours 15 Minutes / Total Time: 3 Hours / Yield: 8 conchas

Ingredients
Concha Dough:

- 1 ¼ tsp ground cinnamon
- 3 tsp active dry yeast
- ½ cup of warm water (110 to 115 degrees F/43 to 46 degrees C)
- ⅓ cup lard
- ¾ cup white sugar
- 4 cups all-purpose flour
- ½ cup lukewarm evaporated milk
- 1 egg
- 1 tsp salt

Flavored Topping Dough:

- 1 cup all-purpose flour
- ½ cup salted butter
- ⅔ cup white sugar
- 1 tsp vanilla extract
- 1 tbsp unsweetened Dutch-processed cocoa powder

Instructions

1. In a large bowl, mix yeast with water. Add 2 cups of flour, sugar, lard, egg, cinnamon, and salt, and mix them in. Mix until it's smooth. To make the dough easy to work with, add enough of the rest of the flour slowly.
2. Place the dough on a lightly floured surface. Knead for around 5 minutes, or until the dough is smooth and elastic. After putting them in a big bowl that has been greased, turn them over so that the greased side is facing up. Cover and let it rise in a warm place for about an hour and a half.
3. Make the topping dough at the same time. Mix butter and sugar until they are fluffy and light. Add flour and mix until mixture is like coarse crumbs. Divide into two equal parts. Add vanilla extract to one part and cocoa powder to the other.
4. Separate the chocolate topping into 4 small balls. Flatten each ball out into a circle. Do the same thing with the vanilla topping.
5. Make 8 equal pieces of concha dough by punching it down. Roll each piece into a ball and put them on a baking sheet that has been greased. Put a chocolate or vanilla circle on top of each ball of dough and smooth it out. Make five or six small cuts across the circle to make the shape of a shell. Cover and let it rise for 45 minutes or until it has doubled in size.
6. Set the oven to 325 degrees F (165 degrees C).
7. Bake conchas for 15 to 20 minutes, or until lightly browned around the edges.

50. Whole Wheat Torta Rolls

Prep Time: 30 Minutes / Cook Time: 12 Minutes / Total Time: 42 Minutes / Yield: 12 Rolls

Ingredients

- 1 tsp Red Star Active Dry Yeast
- 1 ½ cups all-purpose flour
- ½ tsp Red Star Active Dry Yeast
- 2 – 3 cups all-purpose flour
- 1 cup whole wheat pastry flour
- ¾ cup warm water
- 1 ½ cups warm water
- 2 tsp salt
- ¾ cup whole wheat pastry flour

Instructions

1. Put 1 ½ cups of flour, ¾ cup of whole wheat pastry flour, 1 ½ cups of warm water, and ½ teaspoon of yeast in a large bowl. Mix the ingredients together until they are well blended. Leave the bowl on the counter overnight with the cover.
2. Use paddle attachment on a stand mixer, put sponge that has been sitting out overnight, 1 cup whole wheat pastry flour, ¾ cup warm water, 2 tsp salt, and 1 tsp yeast in the bowl. Keep mixing slowly for two minutes. Switch to the dough hook and gradually incorporate 2 cups of all-purpose flour, add more flour as needed to make a soft, sticky dough. Then, knead for 5 minutes. Put in a bowl that has been greased and turn to grease the top. Keep the dough covered and let it rise in a warm place for at least 1 hour, or until it doubles in size.
3. Press the dough down. Leave it alone for 10 minutes with the cover on.
4. Roll out the dough into a 9-by-12-inch rectangle on a floured surface. Make three rows of three 3" x 12" pieces of dough with a pizza cutter. Make four 3-inch squares out of each row.
5. Place the rolls on two non-rimmed baking sheets lined with parchment paper. Cover with non-stick spray-coated plastic wrap. Let rise until the rolls are puffy and a small mark shows up when you lightly touch one of them. This should take about 30 minutes.
6. Heat the oven up to 450°. While the rolls are rising, heat up a pizza stone in the oven.
7. After heating the pizza stone, put the parchment paper with the six rolls on it and bake for 10 to 12 minutes, until the rolls are golden brown. Put them on a wire rack to cool down completely before you eat them. Follow the same steps with the last 6 rolls.

Made in the USA
Columbia, SC
06 April 2025